WITHDRAWN

D1514803

LIVES IN CRISIS

Conflict in Northern Ireland

R. G. GRANT

W

HODDER
Wayland

An imprint of Hodder Children's Books

Copyright © Hodder Wayland 2001

Published in Great Britain in 2001 by
Hodder Wayland, an imprint of Hodder Children's Books.
This edition reprinted in 2002
This book was prepared for Hodder Wayland by Ruth Nason.

Series concept: Alex Woolf
Series design: Carole Binding

British Library Cataloguing in Publication Data
Grant, Reg
   Conflict in Northern Ireland. - (Lives in crisis)
   1.Social conflict - Northern Ireland - History - Juvenile literature
   2.Social conflict - Religious aspects - Juvenile literature
   3.Peace movements - Northern Ireland - Juvenile literature
   4.Northern Ireland - Politics and government - 1949 -
   5.Northern Ireland - History- Juvenile literature
   I.Title
   941.6'082

ISBN 0 7502 3429 6

Printed and bound in Italy by G. Canale & C.S.p.A., Turin

Hodder Children's Books
A division of Hodder Headline Limited
338 Euston Road, London NW1 3BH

Cover (left) and page 1
A masked Catholic child in
the Ardoyne area of
Belfast, July 1996.

Acknowledgements

The Author and Publishers thank the following for their permission to
reproduce photographs: Camera Press: pages 6, 7, 9, 12, 13t, 14, 16, 17t,
20, 25t, 25b, 27, 28, 29t, 31, 32t, 32b, 33t, 33b, 34, 35, 36t, 39, 43, 46,
47; Popperfoto: cover and pages 1, 3, 4, 5, 10, 11t, 11b, 13b, 15, 17b, 19,
21, 22, 29b, 30, 36b, 37, 40, 42, 45, 48, 49t, 49b, 50, 51t, 51b, 52t, 52b,
53t, 53b, 54, 55, 56, 57, 58, 59.

CONTENTS

Flames from a petrol bomb
blaze in a Londonderry
(Derry) street, at the start
of 'the Troubles' in 1969.

WHY DID THEY DIE?

The initials of the Irish Republican Army on a telegraph pole in South Armagh in 1999.

On Saturday, 15 August 1998, British soldiers manning observation posts in Armagh, Northern Ireland, watched two cars drive along the country roads that lead north from the border with southern Ireland. The cars seemed unremarkable and attracted no special attention. But inside were members of an Irish Republican group calling itself the Real IRA, and one of the cars, a stolen maroon Vauxhall Cavalier, was packed with explosives. They were on their way to the small town of Omagh in County Tyrone, to carry out what would prove to be the worst atrocity in 30 years of conflict in Northern Ireland.

The 'Troubles' had started in 1969 with clashes between the Protestant majority and the Catholic minority in Northern Ireland. The Catholic IRA (Irish Republican Army) had subsequently attempted to end British rule in the province by force of arms. In 1998 the IRA was publicly committed to an end to violence, as attempts went ahead to implement a Northern Ireland peace agreement. But IRA men opposed to the agreement had formed the Real IRA and were carrying out terrorist acts in an effort to reignite the conflict.

Cleansing bloodshed

Early in the 20th century, one of the founding fathers of Irish Republicanism, Patrick Pearse, expressed the movement's traditional attitude to violence, which some still hold to today:

'We may make mistakes ... and shoot the wrong people, but bloodshed is a cleansing and sanctifying thing, and the nation which regards it as the final horror has lost its manhood.'
(Quoted in Jeffery ed., *The Divided Province*)

In the early afternoon of 15 August, the Real IRA men parked the maroon Cavalier in the centre of Omagh. After activating a timer linked to the explosives, they got out of the car and walked away. The town was busy with weekend shoppers. Kevin and Philomena Skelton were taking their three daughters to Watterson's clothes store in Market Street to buy school uniforms for the new term. Mary Grimes was celebrating her 65th birthday with a trip to the town, accompanied by her daughter and 18-month-old grand-daughter. Aidan Gallagher, a 21-year-old car mechanic, had decided to go into town to buy some jeans. A party of Spanish schoolchildren on a visit to Northern Ireland had stopped off in Omagh with some Irish friends, including 12-year-old James Barker, 8-year-old Oran Doherty and 12-year-old Sean McLaughlin.

This snapshot of a Spanish visitor to Omagh was taken seconds before the car on the right exploded. The girl's face was blanked out by the police before they released the photo.

Around 2.30 pm, the police received a phone call saying that a bomb had been left near the courthouse at the top of Market Street. By 3.10 they had carried out the difficult task of clearing the area around the courthouse, moving people further down the street. Some shop assistants stepped out of the doors of their shops to see what was going on. Just alongside the maroon car parked in the now crowded part of the street away from the courthouse, a member of the Spanish school party posed for a holiday snap. Seconds later, the car exploded.

Scene of carnage

Dorothy Boyle, who was in Omagh when the bomb went off, described to journalists the terrible scene she witnessed:

'I saw bodies lying everywhere. I saw them being put in bags and being zipped up ... There were people with cuts in their heads, bleeding. There was one boy had half his leg blown off and it was lying there with the wee shoe still on it. He didn't cry or anything. He was just in shock.'
(*Daily Telegraph*, 16 August 1998)

In an instant, the area was reduced to a chaos of glass and rubble. The explosion inflicted terrible burns and blast injuries. Philomena Skelton was killed; so were Mary Grimes, her daughter and granddaughter; James Barker, Oran Doherty, Sean McLaughlin and two of the Spanish school party; Aidan Gallagher; and others like them – ordinary individuals, young and old, who just happened to be in the wrong place at the wrong time. In all, 29 people died and over 200 were injured, many of them seriously. The victims were both Catholics and Protestants – people from both sides of the sectarian divide in Northern Ireland.

The centre of Omagh after the bombing: the men who carried out this attack hoped that the carnage and destruction would disrupt the Northern Ireland peace process.

No healing

Kevin Skelton lost his wife Philomena in the Omagh bombing, in which his three teenage daughters were also injured. Only a metre away from his wife when the bomb went off, Kevin suffered barely a scratch, but the emotional trauma was intense. A year after the tragedy, he told a journalist that he was still plagued by terrifying nightmares:

'I always dream that something happens that separates me from the family and that I can do nothing at all about it ... People keep saying that time heals. Well, it hasn't, not yet, for me.'
(*Daily Telegraph*, 15 August 1999)

Looking to the future

On 15 August 1998 Gary McGillion and his fiancée Donna Marie Keyes were in Omagh shopping for their wedding, which was due to take place the following Saturday. Caught in the full blast of the bomb, Donna Marie suffered horrendous burns; her 21-month-old niece, Breda Devine, was killed. Against the odds, Donna Marie survived, and her battle to recover became a symbol of the determination of the people of Omagh to overcome the tragedy. In March 1999, Gary and Donna Marie were married. Although she still bore terrible scars, Donna Marie was a radiant bride. She said:

'We were not going to let the bombers turn us into bitter people. It would have been easy to feel sorry for ourselves and spend the rest of our lives full of anger and self-pity. I cannot change the past. All I can do is make the best of the future.'
(*Daily Telegraph*, 28 March 1999)

Complex conflict

One immediate reaction to the news of the Omagh bombing was to ask how anyone could carry out such a brutal outrage. Yet in the context of Irish history it was not so extraordinary. Some 3,000 people have been killed in Northern Ireland by bombs or bullets since the late 1960s. Since the start of the 20th century many others have died in violent conflicts in Ireland involving the British, the Catholic Irish and Protestants.

This book will examine the roots of the hatreds and political passions that have torn Ireland apart. It will describe the impact of these events on people's lives, and look at the efforts being made by Irish people, north and south, to escape from their violent history and create a more peaceful future.

Demonstrators in Belfast call for the peace process to continue, after IRA bombings in 1996 threatened a return to full-scale conflict.

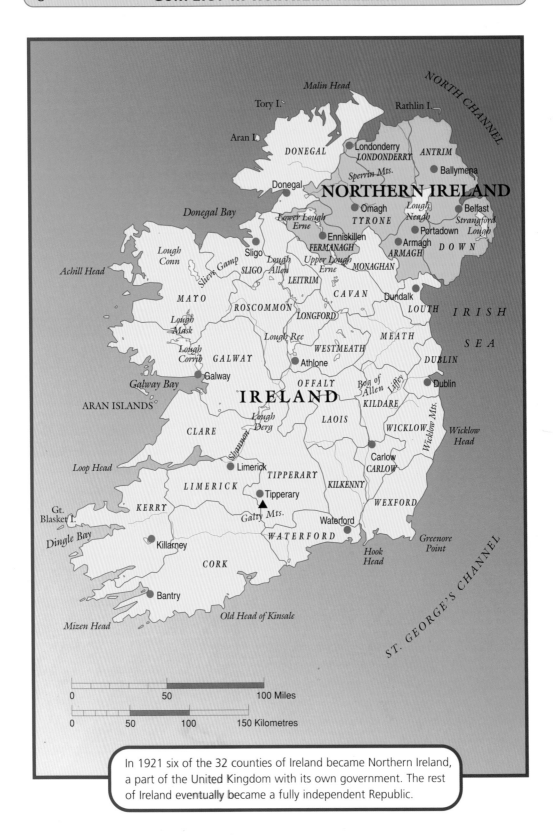

In 1921 six of the 32 counties of Ireland became Northern Ireland, a part of the United Kingdom with its own government. The rest of Ireland eventually became a fully independent Republic.

A TROUBLED HISTORY

The roots of the current conflict in Ireland reach far back into the past. A common sight in Protestant areas of cities in Northern Ireland, for example, is an image of the British King William III (William of Orange) who ruled 300 years ago. Protestant marches every year celebrate events of similar antiquity. Catholic Irish nationalists are often equally fixated on the history of Ireland, which they traditionally see as a long struggle for freedom against oppression by the English, peopled with martyrs and heroes.

English rule

An English army first invaded Ireland in the 12th century, but English rule was not extended over the whole island until 1603. The English generally regarded the Gaelic-speaking inhabitants as 'savages'. In the 16th century relations between the English and the native Irish were further complicated by a religious divide. The Reformation split Christian Europe into Protestants, who rejected the authority of the Pope, and Catholics. England became a Protestant country, but the Irish remained overwhelmingly Catholic.

Although he died in 1702, the mounted image of William of Orange still appears on the walls of Protestant areas of Northern Ireland as a symbol of opposition to Catholics and Catholicism.

The English resorted to a policy of encouraging Protestants to settle in Ireland. These 'plantations' of Protestants were intended to replace a disloyal Catholic Irish population with loyal subjects of the king. Protestant settlement was most dense in Ulster, the province of Ireland closest to Scotland, where most of the settlers came from.

12 July 1999: around 5,000 Orangemen marched through the centre of Portadown, Northern Ireland, to commemorate the Battle of the Boyne.

In 1641 there was a Catholic Irish uprising in which many Ulster Protestants were killed. The uprising was put down with great violence. Irish Catholics suffered an even more decisive setback when the Catholic King James II, driven from the English throne by the Protestant William III in 1688, made Ireland the base for an attempt to regain power. In 1690, William led an army into Ireland and defeated James at the Battle of the Boyne. In the aftermath of this defeat, through much of Ireland Catholics were deprived of their land, which was handed to Protestant landowners. After this the British ruled Ireland with the support of a Protestant 'Anglo-Irish' elite who owned most of the land and controlled the Irish parliament in Dublin. Catholics were barred from voting or holding government jobs, and suffered restrictions in education and the practice of their religion. However, the majority of Ulster Protestants were also denied political rights, because they were 'Dissenters', members of Presbyterian churches that did not conform to the beliefs of the official Protestant Church of Ireland.

United Irishmen

Some of these Ulster Presbyterians played a leading role in the United Irishmen movement which threatened British rule in the 1790s. Led by a Dublin-born Protestant, Wolfe Tone, the United Irishmen called for an independent Irish republic in which 'the common name of Irishman' would replace 'the denominations of Protestant, Catholic and Dissenter'. But such a tolerant attitude was rare. At the same period, fighting between Catholics and Protestants broke out in areas of Ulster, leading to the formation of the Orange Order, a key organization of Ulster Protestantism in its resistance to Catholic influence.

In 1798 a United Irishmen uprising was crushed and Wolfe Tone committed suicide in prison. Two years later, to strengthen its hold on Ireland, the British government abolished the Irish parliament. By the Act of Union, Ireland was declared a part of the United Kingdom of Great Britain and Ireland, sending MPs to the parliament in Westminster, just as Wales and Scotland did.

In Ireland attitudes to the Union soon divided in line with religious allegiance. Most Catholics supported a return to some form of self-government (known as Home Rule), if not

Wolfe Tone (1763-98) led the United Irishmen uprising against British rule.

A mural in a Catholic area of West Belfast expresses the Republican view of Irish history as an unfinished struggle for freedom from British oppression.

Bad harvests typically left Irish families with no money to pay the rent and so they were evicted.

complete independence from British rule, while most Protestants wanted to remain part of the United Kingdom. This divide became more marked as Catholics gradually gained equal political rights. From 1829 Catholics were allowed to be MPs, meaning that any Irish parliament would be dominated by a Catholic majority.

Hunger and nationalism

The Great Famine of 1845-50 has often been seen as a turning point in Irish history. Potato blight caused a catastrophic failure of the potato crop on which much of Ireland's poverty-stricken rural population depended for food. Over a million people are thought to have died in the famine. Between 1845 and 1870 another 3 million Irish emigrated to escape hunger and poverty. Most went to the USA, although many also moved to Britain. The population of Ireland, over 8 million in 1841, was only 4.5 million 50 years later.

Victims of famine

This account appeared in a newspaper in Cork, southern Ireland, during the Great Famine:

'The following is a statement of what I saw yesterday evening on the lands of Toureen. In a cabbage garden I saw ... the bodies of Kate Barry and her two children very lightly covered with earth, the hands and legs of her large body entirely exposed, the flesh completely eaten off by the dogs ...Within about 30 yards, at the opposite side of the road, are two most wretched-looking old houses, with two dead bodies in each ... I need make no comment on this, but ask, are we living in a portion of the United Kingdom?'
(Quoted in Ó Grada, *The Great Irish Famine*)

Many Irish people blamed the British government for the famine and saw the poverty of their country as the result of British rule. Anti-English Irish nationalism found expression in the Fenian movement, an underground organization dedicated to getting the English out, by force if necessary. Foreshadowing the later activities of the IRA, the Fenians brought violence to England, with bomb attacks in Manchester and London. At the same time, in the Westminster parliament, Irish MPs applied pressure for Home Rule.

The predominantly Protestant areas of Ulster increasingly diverged from the rest of Ireland. Industries developed there, especially in the fast-growing city of Belfast, and most Ulster Protestants came to feel that their economic interests lay in remaining a part of the United Kingdom. With these economic interests reinforcing their religious hostility to being ruled by 'Papists', Ulster Protestants took an absolute stand against Home Rule, which they were prepared to resist by force. In 1886 the slogan was launched: 'Ulster will fight and Ulster will be right.'

Above: In the 1880s, Charles Parnell and his Home Rule Party put pressure on the British government to allow Home Rule for Ireland.
Below: Ulster's response to the 1912 Home Rule bill.

Arming for the struggle

In 1912 an Irish Home Rule bill, introduced by the Liberal government, was passed by the House of Commons with the support of Irish MPs. It would have given an Irish government considerable control of its own internal affairs, although it fell far short of offering Ireland full independence. The bill was set to become law in 1914.

Ulster Unionists – Protestants who wanted to retain the Union with Britain – responded by signing a 'solemn league and covenant' that committed them to using 'all means which may be found necessary to defeat the present conspiracy to set up a Home Rule parliament in Ireland'. They formed an Ulster

Irish Volunteers reach out for arms, brought secretly to Dublin Bay in July 1914.

Volunteer Force (UVF) of over 100,000 men who underwent military training, and established a 'provisional government' to run Ulster if Home Rule was declared. This resistance to the British government was supported by the leaders of the opposition Conservative Party and by many officers in the British army, including some of the highest rank.

Both the British government and the Home Rule movement in Ireland were taken aback by the fierceness of the Ulster Unionists' actions. They eventually offered a compromise, allowing the six counties of Ulster that had a Protestant majority to temporarily opt out of Home Rule. But this did not satisfy the Unionists.

In response to the formation of the UVF, Irish people in favour of Home Rule – mostly Catholics – set up the Irish Volunteers as a nationalist paramilitary force. After the Unionists staged a spectacular gun-running operation, landing 25,000 rifles in Ulster, the Irish Volunteers carried out their own illegal landing of arms near Dublin. Ireland was on the brink of civil war.

Fighting for religion

Major Fred Crawford, who organized the shipping of guns to the Protestant Ulster Volunteer Force in 1914, later remembered his high sense of religious purpose in this act of resistance to Home Rule:

'I walked up and down the deck tormented by the thought of all those men waiting for me to bring them the weapons with which to fight for their religion, their liberty and all that was dear to them ... I went into my cabin and threw myself on my knees, and in simple language told God all about it: what this meant to Ulster ...'
(Quoted in Foster, *Modern Ireland*)

War and revolution

The situation was transformed by the outbreak of war in Europe in August 1914. As Britain went to war with Germany, Home Rule was postponed until the conflict should end. The UVF immediately offered to fight for Britain in France, and became part of the British army. The majority of the Irish Volunteers also offered Britain their services, although they were accepted more reluctantly by the British army.

But a minority of the Irish Volunteers, led by a group called the Irish Republican Brotherhood (IRB), rejected fighting for Britain. They were Irish nationalists who saw Britain's involvement in a European war as an opportunity to push for complete independence. Joined by a small left-wing group called the Citizen Army, the IRB planned an uprising for Easter 1916. It proved chaotic and, in practical terms, totally unsuccessful. The rebels seized control of a number of buildings in Dublin and proclaimed an independent republic. They held out for a week against a counter-attack by heavily armed British troops. Several

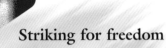

Striking for freedom

Patrick Pearse, the main leader of the Easter Uprising, read out a proclamation on the steps of the Dublin Post Office:

'In the name of God and of the dead generations from which she receives her old tradition of nationhood, Ireland, through us, summons her children to her flag and strikes for her freedom ... We declare the right of the people of Ireland to the ownership of Ireland, and to the unfettered control of Irish destinies ...'

British soldiers at a barricade in Talbot Street, Dublin, during the Easter Uprising, 1916.

British soldiers pick through the rubble in the centre of Dublin after the crushing of the 1916 Easter Uprising. The use of artillery by the British army caused extensive damage.

hundred people died and parts of the city were reduced to rubble before the rebels surrendered.

The uprising enjoyed virtually no public support in Ireland. But as 15 of its leaders were executed, they became instant martyrs in the eyes of the Catholic Irish. The severity of the British repression brought a wave of support for nationalism.

Terrible beauty

The Irish poet W. B. Yeats was one of those who saw the executed leaders of the Easter Uprising as transformed into heroic martyrs through their blood sacrifice. After the executions he wrote a famous poem called 1916, which ends:

'MacDonagh and MacBride
And Connolly and Pearse
Now and in time to be,
Wherever green is worn,
Are changed, changed utterly:
A terrible beauty is born.'

To Ulster Unionists, the Easter Uprising seemed more evidence of the treacherous nature of the Irish Catholics. They contrasted the uprising with another event of 1916, the battle of the Somme in July, when the Ulster Division – chiefly former members of the UVF – lost around 5,000 men in two days' fighting on behalf of Britain. Despite the fact that many thousands of Catholic Irish also fought and gave their lives for the British cause during the First World War, the war strengthened the emotional bond between Ulster Protestants and Britain, while it brought an increasing alienation of Irish Catholics from British rule. The scene was set for the division of Ireland.

A DIVIDED ISLAND

In December 1918, after the end of the First World War, a general election was held in the United Kingdom. Sinn Fein, a political party calling for an independent Irish republic, won an overwhelming victory throughout Catholic Ireland. The Sinn Fein MPs refused to take their seats in the Westminster parliament, instead setting themselves up as an Irish parliament, the Dail Eireann, in Dublin. They went on to behave like an independent government, establishing their own courts and administration.

The Irish Volunteers became known as the Irish Republican Army (IRA), which embarked on an assassination campaign against policemen of the Royal Irish Constabulary – who were mostly Irish Catholics. The British authorities responded by recruiting British ex-servicemen for duties in Ireland – the 'Black and Tans' and the Auxiliaries. A vicious campaign of terror and counter-terror followed. When the IRA guerrillas carried out

Five rifles protrude from a steel window-shield at a Royal Irish Constabulary police barracks, 1919.

The Auxiliaries were British ex-servicemen recruited to fight the IRA in 1920-21. Here their armoured car is covered with wire netting as protection against bomb-throwers.

Rebel songs

The events of the Anglo-Irish War are glorified in popular Irish ballads. One of the most famous is *Kevin Barry*. It celebrates an 18-year-old IRA volunteer hanged by the British in 1920 for taking part in an ambush in which a soldier was killed. To the British he was a murderer, but to Republicans he was a hero and martyr. The song begins:

'In Mountjoy jail one Monday morning
High upon the gallows tree
Kevin Barry gave his young life
For the cause of liberty.

'But a lad of eighteen summers
Yet there's no one can deny
As he walked to death that morning
He proudly held his head on high.'
(Quoted in O'Connor, *The Troubles*)

ambushes or assassinations, the Black and Tans and the 'Auxis' responded by burning houses and arbitrary killing. More than 750 people died in this Anglo-Irish War between 1919 and 1921.

Partition and civil war

Meanwhile, in 1920 the British government pushed through a Government of Ireland Act, which effectively divided Ireland in two. There were to be separate administrations in Belfast (running six counties in Ulster) and Dublin (running the other 26 counties of Ireland). Both would remain under the overall control of the British government. A Council of Ireland was supposed to look after matters of common interest to both parts of Ireland. The Belfast parliament was set up at Stormont in the summer of 1921, but the deal was not acceptable to Irish leaders in Dublin. A ceasefire was declared and, after lengthy negotiations, in December 1921 Irish representatives agreed a treaty with the British giving the 26 counties a similar status to a dominion such as Canada – effectively independent, but still owing allegiance to the British crown.

This treaty led to civil war in what became known as the Irish Free State. Anti-treaty Republicans, led by Eamon de Valera and including the majority of the IRA, rejected the idea of an oath of allegiance to the British king. On this symbolic issue Irish fought Irish in a civil war even more bitter and destructive than the war with England that had preceded it. Some 4,000 people died before the anti-treaty forces gave up the struggle in May 1923.

Eamon de Valera (centre right) reviews IRA 'Irregulars' in 1922. De Valera led the anti-treaty fight in the civil war of 1922-23, but later turned against the IRA.

Violent birth

Violence also marked the birth of Northern Ireland. Inevitably, Protestant voters elected a Unionist majority to the Belfast parliament. Soon after, in July 1921, Protestant mobs attacked Catholic areas of Belfast, burning down houses, and many Catholics were forced out of their jobs by hostile Protestant workmates. Meanwhile the IRA began a campaign of kidnappings, ambushes, assassinations and bombings in Northern Ireland, in order to complete – as they saw it – the liberation of Ireland from British rule. The Unionist

Family tradition

The tradition of republicanism and IRA activism was handed down from the time of the Anglo-Irish War and partition to the present day. Eamon Larkin, a member of Sinn Fein in Northern Ireland in the 1990s, made the point:

'I was born into it. The man that took me into the Republican movement was Peter McAteer ..., my father's company captain [in the IRA] from the 1920s. That tradition was in families.'
(Quoted in Harnden, *Bandit Country*)

administration responded by forming the B-Specials, a force of armed police largely recruited from former members of the UVF. A Special Powers Act gave the authorities powers similar to those of martial law, and suspected terrorists were interned – that is, imprisoned without trial.

The brutal violence continued until 1923, with many killings on both sides. It confirmed every prejudice dividing Catholics and Protestants in the North. The Unionists were convinced that Catholics were disloyal 'Fenians', bent on overthrowing the state, while the Catholics saw themselves as the defenceless victims of Protestant authorities which had either allowed or directly carried out sectarian attacks.

Some border areas of the six counties had a large Catholic majority, and it was widely expected that these would be transferred to the Free State by a border commission in 1925. But the border was never adjusted – another contribution to the Catholics' sense of injustice. Catholics believed that Northern Ireland was simply the largest area that could be guaranteed to have a permanent Protestant majority.

Catholic and Protestant states

The way the new Irish Free State shaped up confirmed Ulster Protestant fears and prejudices. The Catholic Church was given effective control of education and social policy. Divorce was

Leinster House in Dublin has been home to the Irish parliament since 1922.

banned and unmarried mothers were harshly treated. The word of the parish priest was law in many country villages and towns. The Protestant minority in the South was not persecuted, but dwindled from about 1 in 10 to 1 in 30 of the population. This was partly because the Catholic Church ruled that children of marriages between a Protestant and a Catholic must be brought up as Catholics.

There was no reconciliation with Britain. Irish governments tried to eradicate the legacy of British rule, notably by trying (unsuccessfully) to revive Gaelic as the national language in place of English. Irish schools taught a simplistic nationalist version of history with the English cast as the villains. The remaining links with Britain were weakened by a new constitution in 1937, and abolished in 1949, when Ireland became a republic and left the British Commonwealth.

In Northern Ireland, by contrast, the Unionist government took every opportunity to stress their identification with

Protestant fears

Sir Richard Bates, a Unionist politician, expressed the feelings of many Ulster Protestants when he said in 1938:

'So long as we live there will always be the danger of Home Rule or merging into the Free State. We will never get rid of it ... All we want is to live our lives as God has placed us here. Yet we have this continual menace at our doors – a menace which will last as long as we live.'
(Quoted in Hennessey, *A History of Northern Ireland*)

Stormont was built in parkland outside Belfast in the late 1920s to house the Northern Ireland parliament.

Britain, for example by flying the Union flag. They also stressed the province's religious identity. In 1932 Northern Ireland prime minister Lord Craigavon declared: 'We are a Protestant parliament and a Protestant state.' The Catholics who made up one third of the population of Northern Ireland played no part in its central government. The nationalist MPs they elected to the Stormont parliament had no influence, given the permanent Unionist majority elected by Protestants.

British commitment

Britain's commitment to Northern Ireland became more solid over time. Early in the Second World War (1939-45), the British government offered to accept the principle of a united Ireland in return for the use of Irish ports by its warships. But nothing came of this approach and Ireland remained neutral. By contrast, Northern Ireland contributed substantially to the British war effort and Belfast suffered heavily from bombing by the German Luftwaffe. According to Britain's wartime prime minister, Winston Churchill, the bond between Britain and Northern Ireland was now unbreakable because it had been 'tempered by fire'. In 1949, after Ireland left the Commonwealth, the British parliament passed an Ireland Act which stated that 'in no event will Northern Ireland or any part thereof cease to be part of ... the United Kingdom without the consent of the Parliament of Northern Ireland.'

After the war Northern Ireland benefited greatly from the new 'welfare state' set up in the United Kingdom. Although always poor by British standards, by the 1950s people living in the province were clearly, on average, much better off than people in the Irish Republic – where, for example, running water was still rare in rural homes. It seemed to Ulster Unionists that southern

In 1952 this photograph illustrated a news article entitled 'Eire Land of Bachelors'. Thirty-eight year-old Patrick Moran was one of seven bachelors living in one lane in County Leitrim. All the young women were said to have left the Irish countryside for the cities and good wages of Britain and the USA.

Ireland was a place of poverty and backwardness where Catholic superstition held sway. Even Catholics in the North grew away from their co-religionists south of the border, with different experiences and expectations. British education reforms allowed some Catholics to increase their educational status, and a Catholic middle class began to develop.

IRA campaigns

The Irish Republic theoretically laid claim to govern all of Ireland – this was written into the Irish constitution. But although the existence of this claim stoked up Unionist fears, there was little or no real desire on the part of the Irish government to achieve unification. This was true even after de Valera, who had led the anti-treaty side in the civil war, became prime minister in 1932. De Valera's Fianna Fáil party and Fine Gael, the party descended from the pro-treaty side in the civil conflict, dominated Irish politics. Sinn Fein was left as a small extremist movement, acting as the political voice of the IRA. The IRA and Sinn Fein remained actively committed to the goal of 'driving the invader from the soil of Ireland'. But from the 1930s they had the support of only a small minority among Irish Catholics. The IRA was a banned organization south of the border as well as in Northern Ireland.

In 1939 the IRA mounted a bombing campaign against targets on the British mainland. One bomb killed five people in a Coventry shopping street, but the campaign was then eclipsed by the outbreak of the Second World War. The next major IRA offensive did not come until 1956, when the organization launched a 'border

Better off in the UK

Many Catholic nationalists in the 1950s found it hard to accept that they were benefiting from British rule. Social Democratic and Labour Party activist Ben Caraher said of Catholics in South Armagh:

'It was strange for the older people to see their children benefiting, going to grammar school. They couldn't say that was a bad thing. The upwardly mobile benefited most from the welfare state, the benefits came from the fact that we were part of the UK. But anyone who overtly said something like that was considered a traitor ...'
(Quoted in O'Connor, *In Search of a State*)

A terrorist's duty

Sentenced at the Old Bailey in 1939 to 20 years' prison for bomb attacks in London, IRA man Gerard Lyons told the court:

'I believe it is a just and Christian thing to try and overthrow tyranny. It is a Christian thing to strike at it and the British government have tyrannized Ireland. While it exists it is the duty of every Irishman to try and overthrow this tyranny, and I believe I have done my duty to my country.'
(Quoted in Kee, *The World We Left Behind*)

A child's fears

The IRA campaign of the 1950s had little practical effect, but it did frighten many Protestants. Jeffrey Glenn remembered how it affected him:

'As a young child, I used to look carefully under my bed every night before saying my prayers. The IRA campaign of the fifties was in full swing and I was checking for bombs. Even if I couldn't see one, I still lay quaking with fear for what seemed like hours every night ... The weeks passed and I didn't get blown up but the ideas of being under siege to the IRA and of being killed by them were among my earliest memories.'
(Quoted in Holliday, *Children of "the Troubles"*)

war' against Northern Ireland, chiefly attacking customs posts and police stations. The campaign drew little support from Catholics north or south of the border and petered out long before it was formally abandoned in 1962.

Avoiding contamination

In 1951 Bishop Farren advised Catholic parents in Northern Ireland to keep their children away from Protestant dance-halls, where 'the standard of purity was not as high as it was among Catholics'. The bishop warned:

'If you allow your children to be contaminated by those not of the Fold then you can expect nothing but disaster ... It is too late whenever a dangerous friendship is formed which may lead your girl along the road to hell ...'
(Quoted in Hennessey, *A History of Northern Ireland*)

Problems and prejudice

By the 1960s, when the present 'Troubles' began, Northern Ireland was a place in which two communities lived separate lives side by side. Catholics and Protestants were often neighbours in the same streets, but their children went to separate schools and learned radically different versions of Irish history. They also, of course, worshipped at separate churches – church-going was far more common than in Britain. Leaders of both communities did their best to discourage young Catholics and Protestants from mixing with one another. Most Catholics thought of themselves as 'Irish', while most Protestants described themselves as 'British' or 'Ulstermen'.

Two homes in Londonderry (Derry) at the end of the 1960s: (top) a four-roomed house in the Protestant area was home to six adults and three young children; (bottom) the home of a family with five children in the Catholic area. Although living conditions for both Protestant and Catholic working-class people were poor, on average Protestants were more prosperous and better housed.

Catholics and Protestants shared problems of poverty, unemployment and poor housing, but the Catholics suffered the more from all three. Most businesses were run by Protestants, and Protestant workers occupied most of the better-paid skilled jobs. An overwhelming majority of the police – the Royal Ulster Constabulary (RUC) – were Protestant, as were the majority in the upper levels of the civil service. Some local government districts were run by Catholics, although notoriously the manipulation of voting districts meant that Londonderry (Derry) had a Protestant council although the majority of the population was Catholic. Where Protestants ran local councils, Catholics believed that they were discriminated against in the allocation of council housing.

'Employ good Protestant lads'

There was a long history of discrimination against Catholics in employment. At a gathering of members of the Orange Order in 1932, Unionist politician Sir Basil Brooke said:

'There are a great number of Protestants and Orangemen who employ Roman Catholics. I feel I can speak freely on this subject as I have not a Roman Catholic about my own place. I appreciate the great difficulty experienced by some of you in procuring suitable Protestant labour but I would point out that Roman Catholics are endeavouring to get in everywhere. I appeal to Loyalists therefore, wherever possible, to employ good Protestant lads and lassies.'
(Quoted in Hennessey, *A History of Northern Ireland*)

Most Protestants had a clear sense of superiority over Catholics. In the summer 'marching season' each year, Protestants paraded through the streets with banners celebrating historic victories over the Catholic foe – often marching through the middle of predominantly Catholic districts. But they also feared the Catholics. Their anxieties focused on the higher Catholic birthrate, which in the long term threatened the Protestant majority in Northern Ireland; possible attack by the IRA; and the continued claim by the Republic to rule the whole of Ireland.

The grievances of the Catholic population and the fears of the Protestants were to produce an explosion of violence at the end of the 1960s.

Owning Ulster

Professor Denis O'Donohue, an Irish academic brought up in Northern Ireland in the 1940s, claimed that the difference between a Protestant and Catholic was instantly visible:

'In the North a Protestant walks with an air of possession and authority ... he walks as if he owns the place, which indeed he does. A Catholic walks as if he were there on suffrance.'
(Quoted in Somerville-Large, *Irish Voices*)

FROM CIVIL RIGHTS TO STREET WARFARE

In the 1960s, it seemed to many people in Northern Ireland –
both Catholics and Unionists – that changes were needed.
Captain Terence O'Neill, Northern Ireland prime minister
from 1963, tried to introduce reforms and to improve relations
with the Republic. But his actions only excited the hostility of
some Protestants, including Ian Paisley, who became the
leading spokesman for resistance to any concessions to
Catholics. In 1966 a Protestant paramilitary group 'declared
war' on the IRA and murdered two Catholics in Belfast.

It was in this already tense and unstable situation that the
Northern Ireland Civil Rights Association (NICRA) was
created to campaign for reform in 1967. Its demands included
equal rights for Catholics in public housing, electoral reform
to create genuine democracy, a general end to discrimination
on grounds of religion and the disbandment of the feared

Northern Ireland politician
Reverend Ian Paisley
addresses a crowd of
Protestant admirers. Since
the 1960s Paisley has been
one of the most outspoken
opponents of any
compromise with Catholics.

Liberating struggle

Brought up in the Catholic Bogside district of Derry, writer Nell McCafferty saw the civil rights struggle as liberating for Catholic housewives:

'They burst out of their homes ... and spent their Sundays marching around the city, demanding freedom, just like the men and the children. They joined in the chant for votes, houses and jobs, carried banners, sat down defiantly in the roadway when the RUC blocked the route, helped build barricades, inhaled tear gas, broke the law for the first time in their adult lives, and agreed there was no time to go home to make the supper.'
(McCafferty, *Peggy Deery*)

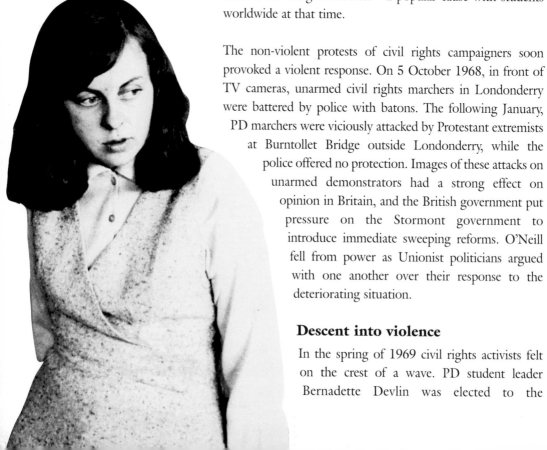

Fiery Catholic activist Bernadette Devlin was elected to the Westminster parliament in 1969, aged 21.

B-Specials. The leading civil rights activists were mostly middle-class liberal Catholics, although some Republicans with IRA connections joined in. A student group called People's Democracy (PD) was also formed, advocating some kind of left-wing revolution – a popular cause with students worldwide at that time.

The non-violent protests of civil rights campaigners soon provoked a violent response. On 5 October 1968, in front of TV cameras, unarmed civil rights marchers in Londonderry were battered by police with batons. The following January, PD marchers were viciously attacked by Protestant extremists at Burntollet Bridge outside Londonderry, while the police offered no protection. Images of these attacks on unarmed demonstrators had a strong effect on opinion in Britain, and the British government put pressure on the Stormont government to introduce immediate sweeping reforms. O'Neill fell from power as Unionist politicians argued with one another over their response to the deteriorating situation.

Descent into violence

In the spring of 1969 civil rights activists felt on the crest of a wave. PD student leader Bernadette Devlin was elected to the

Westminster parliament, at 21 years old the youngest MP in modern times. But the more successful the civil rights movement seemed to be, the more it awakened Protestant fears. In August 1969 the tension erupted into violence on a scale not seen for almost half a century.

The trouble began on 12 August in Derry, on the occasion of the Apprentice Boys' parade, an annual Protestant march. Clashes between Catholics on one side and Protestants and the RUC on the other developed into full-scale riots. Catholics barricaded themselves into the Bogside district and fought off

The annual Apprentice Boys' parade in Londonderry on 12 August 1969 sparked off riots that marked the beginning of the Troubles.

One of the barricades hastily thrown together by Catholics in the Bogside area of Derry on 12-13 August 1969.

Burnt out

A Catholic woman recalled how, as a child, she witnessed the effects of a Protestant attack on a Catholic street in Belfast in August 1969:

'I remember running down our path and looking down the street and seeing women and children running along ... in their pyjamas and nightdresses with the light behind them, the flames, wee black running figures. They had to jump from the backs of their houses on the Crumlin Road ... because their houses were being shot at first and then they were being burnt out, in the early hours of the morning ... They were in mortal terror.'
(Quoted in O'Connor, *In Search of a State*)

British soldiers deployed in Belfast in mid-August 1969 begin to dismantle a barricade put up by local Catholics to protect themselves against Protestant rioters.

attempts by police with armoured cars and tear gas to enter what was declared 'Free Derry'. On 14 August the violence spread to Belfast. Protestant mobs rampaged through Catholic areas, burning down several hundred houses. Eight people were killed. The violence stopped only when British troops were deployed on the streets.

The British soldiers were warmly welcomed by most Catholics, who believed they had been the victims of a murderous onslaught by Protestant extremists, with the active

collaboration of the RUC and B-Specials. Protestants, on the other hand, were convinced that they had defeated an attempted Republican uprising, aimed at the overthrow of the Northern Ireland state. There was Protestant outrage when the Irish taoiseach (prime minister) Jack Lynch reacted to the events by calling for UN intervention and declaring that the unification of Ireland offered the only long-term solution.

Rebirth of the IRA

For a time it seemed that the situation might quieten down. There was little violence for almost a year after the deployment of British troops. The British government imposed reforms on the Unionist government, including the disbanding of the B-Specials and the disarming of the RUC. But Britain stopped short of taking over direct control of Northern Ireland, and promised that there was no question of the unification of Ireland without the consent of Northern Ireland's Protestant majority. This attempt at an even-handed approach satisfied neither Catholics nor Protestants. Fears and hatreds simmered on in the inflammable working-class districts of Belfast and Derry, where unemployment and poor housing contributed to the discontent.

Meanwhile the IRA, which had not played a significant role in the events of August 1969, began to revive. A split in the organization led to the creation of the Provisional IRA, a breakaway group totally committed to an armed struggle to drive the British 'occupying forces' out of Northern Ireland. At first the 'Provos' numbered only a few dozen individuals with very limited armament. But as Catholics became increasingly hostile to the British army and fearful of renewed Protestant attacks, the organization began to grow and developed a reputation for providing Catholic areas with an effective defence.

The leaders of the Provisional IRA in 1972: (left to right) Martin McGuinness, David O'Connell, Sean MacStiofain and Seamus Twomey.

British soldiers confront Catholic women on the streets of Belfast. At first generally welcomed by Catholics, the soldiers soon became the object of hostility and anger.

Civilians are caught up in the fighting as a British army patrol comes under sniper fire in Belfast.

Turning against the army

By mid-1970, many Catholics had come to see British soldiers not as a defence against the Protestants, but as tools of the province's Protestant rulers. This was almost inevitable as the army took on a policing role that included the protection of Protestant marches. Pitched battles between rioters armed with petrol bombs and soldiers with rubber bullets and CS gas occurred with increasing frequency. Soon the Provisionals joined in, shooting at British soldiers – the first soldier to die in the Troubles was killed in February 1971. The British army

A man is made to stand against a wall during a search of the Catholic Falls Road area of Belfast by a British army patrol in 1970.

Catholic women bang dustbin lids on the pavement to warn of the approach of British soldiers.

responded by searching entire Catholic districts for arms, entering every house and sometimes tearing up floorboards. Being stopped and searched became a standard experience for young Catholics. Inevitably, as gun battles developed, innocent people were occasionally killed by British bullets, further fuelling Catholic outrage.

In 1971 the Provisional IRA was able to launch a sustained campaign to end British and Unionist rule in Northern Ireland. As well as attacks on the security forces, including the newly formed Ulster Defence Regiment (UDR), it began

Tough measures

Paddy Devlin, a Catholic Stormont MP opposed to the IRA, described the effect of the British army's action in the Catholic Falls Road area of Belfast in 1970:

'Homes were raided and ransacked at random. Pedestrians were halted and questioned as they walked innocently along the streets. The measures intensified as more and more troops poured in ... Overnight the population turned from neutral or even sympathetic support for the military to outright hatred of everything related to the security forces ... I witnessed voters and workers ... turn against us to join the Provisionals.'
(Quoted in Hennessey, *A History of Northern Ireland*)

Force is the only way

Writing in the Republican newspaper *An Phoblacht* in 1970, Provisional IRA leader Sean MacStiofain said he was 'sorry for anyone's death', but justified the killing of members of the security forces. He wrote:

'As for condemning force, England could not hold any part of Ireland except by military force. When that force was exercised against the population, the troops who exercised it became legitimate targets for Republican resistance fighters.'
(Quoted in Hennessey, *A History of Northern Ireland*)

bomb attacks designed to cripple the province's economy – most of the businesses were owned by Protestants. The Unionist government pushed for ever stronger action by the British army to restore order, but every extra crackdown brought more recruits for the Provisionals.

Shop assistants clearing away broken glass became a daily scene in Belfast as the IRA conducted its bombing offensive in the early 1970s.

High on fighting

There is no doubt that many of the young IRA volunteers who took part in the armed conflict actually enjoyed it. A man who joined the IRA as a teenager in 1971 had fond memories of fighting in South Armagh:

'Guerrilla warfare is a great thing; it's just hit and run ... We didn't really think of killing or being killed; in later years you might think about it but at the time it was all a high. There was a feeling of great exhilaration after an operation. We'd go back and wait for the news to hear the damage we'd done.'
(Quoted in Harnden, *'Bandit Country'*)

Loyal to the Crown

In a newspaper article published in 1970, Protestant leader Ian Paisley explained how he could call himself loyal to Britain, while at the same time resisting the policies of the British government:

'Our flag is the Union Jack, and I think that declares exactly where we stand. I believe that Ulster's future is with Great Britain, but I distinguish between loyalty to the Throne and our attitude towards any particular political party. The voters of Ulster owe no allegiance whatsoever to the [British] government ... but they still claim to be loyal citizens because their allegiance is to the Crown and Constitution ...'
(Quoted in Hennessey, *A History of Northern Ireland*)

Internment to Bloody Sunday

In August 1971, under pressure from the Unionists, the British government agreed to the introduction of internment (imprisonment without trial), the traditional weapon against the IRA (see page 20). It was the moment when the situation started to slip completely out of control. More than 300 people were arrested in army raids on Catholic districts – many of them innocent of any crime. There were allegations that internees were mistreated or even tortured. Violence broke out on an unprecedented scale, as Catholic rioters and snipers took on the army, while Protestants joined in the fighting, attacking Catholic streets and burning houses. In the five months after internment was introduced 143 people were killed in Northern Ireland. The rural border area of South Armagh – known as 'Bandit Country' – became a scene of guerrilla warfare, with gun battles between the army and the Provisional IRA. Some areas of Belfast and Derry were 'no-go areas' for the army, closed off by barricades and openly policed by armed and hooded Provisionals.

Hooded gunmen of the Provisional IRA man a checkpoint at the entrance to a 'no-go area', the Bogside in Derry in 1972.

Bloody Sunday, 30 January 1972: civil rights protesters march through Londonderry.

Crosses are carried for those killed by British soldiers on Bloody Sunday.

The rise of the 'men of violence' was regarded with horror by many Catholics. The Social Democratic and Labour Party (SDLP), set up in 1970, advocated improved rights for Catholics and the eventual unification of Ireland through non-violent means. However, when an attempt was made to revive the civil rights campaign there were tragic results. On 30 January 1972, in Londonderry, 14 Catholics were shot dead by British paratroopers after a civil rights march had led to rioting. This 'Bloody Sunday' massacre shocked world opinion. In Dublin, a mob burned down the British embassy.

In the spring of 1972 the IRA campaign reached a new level of intensity. There were 40 bomb explosions in two days. Protestant paramilitary groups also organized and expanded as law and order disintegrated. The two main groups were the Ulster Defence Association (UDA), soon claiming some 50,000 members, and a smaller group taking the name of

Voice of hate

Writing in the newspaper of the paramilitary UDA in the early 1970s,
a woman expressed the extreme hatred felt by some Protestants as the
IRA campaign of bombings and shootings went on:

'I have reached the stage where I no longer have any compassion for
ANY NATIONALIST, man, woman, or child. I have been driven
against my better feelings and the way my mum and dad brought me up
to take the decision ... IT IS THEM OR US ... If I had a flamethrower
I would roast the slimy excreta which pass for human beings ...'
(Quoted in Hennessey, *A History of Northern Ireland*)

the Ulster Volunteer Force (UVF) from the past organization.
The UDA staged marches in military uniform and made public
statements about the number of weapons they had – in effect
threatening that, if Britain withdrew, the Catholics would find
themselves on the losing side in a civil war.

Women of the Protestant
UDA on the march in July
1972. Such uniformed
marches were staged to
impress the British
government and Catholics
with Protestants' readiness
to fight.

End of Unionist rule

After 50 years of rule in Northern Ireland, however, the
Unionist government at Stormont was now doomed. In
March 1972 the British government took over direct control of

the province. In theory this was a temporary measure, but it was obvious that Britain would never hand Northern Ireland back to exclusive Unionist rule. If any kind of durable peace was to be restored, it would have to be based on a compromise with Catholic nationalists.

The British government's most pressing immediate concern was to stem the rising tide of IRA violence. They decided to explore the possibility of a deal with the IRA. In June 1972 a ceasefire was arranged and Provisional IRA leaders, including Gerry Adams and Martin McGuinness, were flown to London for secret talks. But as their minimum demand was for a total withdrawal of British forces by a fixed date, talks quickly ended. The following month the ceasefire also came to an end.

On the afternoon of 21 July 1972, known as Bloody Friday, 19 bombs exploded in Belfast city centre in one hour. Nine people were killed and 130 injured. Television images of the remains of bodies being scooped into plastic bags shocked all who saw them.

IRA loses support

By this time opposition to the IRA among the Catholic community was growing. This was partly a consequence of the experience of being ruled by gunmen. Within the areas they

Rule of fear

The IRA used the threat of violence to stop Catholics working for or in any way having business with the police or the army. RUC constable Sam Malcomson recalled his experience as a policeman in South Armagh in the early 1970s:

'There was a shop in Crossmaglen where we would go in to buy our newspapers and milk. Then we noticed the shopkeeper being very hesitant ... This woman's attitude suggested to me that she wanted to say: "We've been threatened, we've been told not to serve you." We then made a decision that we wouldn't put her life at risk by coming into her shop any more.'
(Quoted in Harnden, *'Bandit Country'*)

Awful stuff

A Catholic woman from Fermanagh expressed the difficulty some traditional nationalists had as the death toll from the IRA campaign mounted:

'I came from strong Republican roots. At the beginning I felt responsible for every single thing that was done, the IRA car bombs in the early seventies, all that awful stuff ... These were my people blowing the legs off human beings, and I felt bad.'
(Quoted in O'Connor, *In Search of a State*)

controlled, the Provisionals imposed vicious punishments on people who stepped out of line, from petty criminals to those they accused of being 'collaborators'. Punishments included the tarring-and-feathering of girls accused of being friendly with British soldiers. Catholics also shared with Protestants in the terror and disruption spread by the IRA bombing campaign.

The change in mood allowed the British army to seize the initiative. Soon after the Bloody Friday bombings, British soldiers moved into the no-go areas in force and established a permanent presence there. This was a decisive moment, because it halted the rising tide of violence. In 1972 there were 467 deaths in the Northern Ireland conflict. The following year deaths fell to little over half that level. But not even a glimmer of a solution to the conflict was in sight.

A child in Belfast, photographed in 1972 as bombs exploded all around.

THE LONG HAUL

After Britain established direct rule over Northern Ireland in 1972, it began to look for a political deal that would restore a devolved government at Stormont. The solution that took shape the following year was for a power-sharing executive – in other words, despite being the majority, Unionists were obliged to share places in government with the minority Catholics. To conciliate Catholic nationalism, there also had to be an 'Irish dimension'. The Sunningdale agreement of December 1973 provided for a Council of Ireland, with ministers and an assembly drawn from north and south of the border.

Although moderate Unionist leaders supported Sunningdale, a large number of Protestants saw the Council of Ireland as a step on the road to a takeover of Northern Ireland by the Irish Republic – their ultimate nightmare. In May 1974, an alliance of Protestant workers' representatives, Loyalist paramilitaries and Unionist politicians organized a general strike to stop the implementation of the Sunningdale agreement. It brought Northern Ireland to a halt. Loyalists also spread terror to the Irish Republic, detonating car bombs in Dublin and Monaghan that left 33 people dead. The British government was faced with a choice between breaking the strike by force and climbing down. It climbed down. The power-sharing

Belfast, 21 May 1974: supporters of the Protestant workers' strike form a barrier to stop traffic. The strike destroyed the chance of a political settlement based on concessions to the Catholics.

executive and the Sunningdale agreement were abandoned. Direct rule of Northern Ireland from Westminster continued because of the impossibility of finding any other arrangement that could work.

Protestant killings

The anger and anxiety of Protestants found sinister expression in a campaign of sectarian murder – the random killing of Catholics. In the period from 1972 to 1976, Loyalist groups committed more than 500 murders. The notorious 'Shankill Butchers', associated with the UVF, specialized in abducting their victims, torturing them and finishing them off with meat cleavers. The IRA responded with their own sectarian killings, including the murder of 10 Protestant workers at Kingsmill, County Armagh, in January 1976.

The horrors of sectarian murder contributed to the effective segregation of Northern Ireland society. Between 1969 and the mid-1970s, tens of thousands of people fled mixed Catholic-Protestant districts to seek safety among their co-religionists. Some were driven out by incendiary attacks, others scared out by threats or a general sense of fear. Many who refused to budge ended up swelling the death statistics, often gunned

Learning to hate

Alistair Little is a Protestant who was imprisoned at the age of 17 for murdering a Catholic. Later in life, when he had completely changed his views, he remembered the key incident that had made him join a Protestant paramilitary group. When he was 15, a local UDR soldier was shot dead in his home by IRA gunmen. Little went to the funeral:

'I wasn't prepared for the screams of the soldier's daughter when her father's coffin was lifted on to the shoulders of the coffin bearers ... I began to cry. I could see other people crying, even grown men ... I was frightened, I was angry, and I vowed that if I ever got the opportunity to take revenge on the IRA, on Catholics, and their community I would take that opportunity.'
(Quoted in Holliday, *Children of "the Troubles"*)

Northern Ireland 'Peace People' at a rally in Trafalgar Square, London, November 1976: (left to right) Betty Williams, the US folk singer Joan Baez, Caran McKeown, Jane Ewart-Biggs (whose husband was assassinated when he was British ambassador in Ireland) and Mairead Corrigan.

down on their doorsteps. Although Protestants also suffered in this way, by far the majority of those driven from their homes were Catholics.

In 1976 an attempt to overcome the religious divide and end the cycle of violence was launched by two women from the Andersonstown area of Belfast, Betty Williams and Mairead Corrigan. The movement, later known as the Peace People, began as an emotional reaction to the death of three children, run over by an IRA getaway car. The women organized protests in which Catholics and Protestants marched side by side demanding an end to violence. Many former neighbours, separated by the Troubles, re-established contact across the sectarian divide. Williams and Corrigan were awarded the Nobel Peace Prize for their efforts, but in the end the movement had little long-term effect. It showed that a strong desire for peace existed in Northern Ireland, but offered no solution to the problems that had caused the conflict.

The struggle goes on

The IRA certainly had no intention of giving up the armed struggle for their ideal of a united Ireland. In 1973 the Provisionals took their war to mainland Britain, carrying out a string of bomb attacks in British cities. The worst atrocity occurred in Birmingham in November 1974, when two bombs left in crowded pubs killed 19 people. Such attacks were to continue sporadically for more than two decades.

In 1975 hopes were raised by a lengthy IRA ceasefire. This controversially involved a measure of collaboration between the British army and IRA men in an effort to avoid incidents that might spark a renewal of fighting. As in 1972, there were talks between representatives of Britain and the IRA. But as long as the IRA remained committed to achieving a complete British withdrawal from Northern Ireland there were no serious grounds for a deal, and the terrorist campaign was inevitably soon renewed.

Acceptable violence

By the late 1970s, the security forces had made considerable progress in reducing the violence in Northern Ireland to what was deemed an 'acceptable' level. This was achieved partly by measures that caused great inconvenience to local people – for example, by fencing off city centres and carrying out security checks at entry points. But there were also improvements in intelligence, which enabled the security forces to tackle both Republican and Loyalist paramilitaries more effectively.

From 1977, the number of murders carried out by Loyalists declined sharply – partly because Protestants felt that the threat of a unified Ireland had receded. The IRA was also unable to maintain as high a level of operations as in

British soldiers on patrol near the border with the Republic: by the late 1970s, the IRA was more active in rural areas than in the cities.

Getting used to it

Jeffrey Glenn, a Protestant from the Belfast suburbs, described getting used to living with the Troubles:

'All around me bombs and incendiaries destroyed office blocks, hotels, theatres and shops, city streets, and eventually whole town centres ... Lots of people got shot. Roads were closed. There were army checkpoints and soldiers everywhere ... whole towns were cordoned off at night by "security gates". "Civilian searchers" checked your pockets each time you went into a shop ... Yet, after a few years, all this seemed quite unremarkable. I even began to try to persuade friends and relatives from outside Ireland to come over and visit. "It's not that bad," I would say ...'
(Quoted in Holliday, *Children of "the Troubles"*)

the early 1970s, although attacks continued to take their toll of the security forces. The worst single incident was on 27 August 1979, when 18 British soldiers were killed in an ambush at Warrenpoint, County Down. On the same day as this attack, the Queen's cousin, Earl Mountbatten, and three other people were killed when their boat was blown up at Mullaghmore in the Irish Republic, where the Earl was holidaying. Such spectacular atrocities, however, brought the IRA no nearer to achieving their political goals and drew fierce condemnation from many Catholics.

Britain worked to restore a normal system of law and order in Northern Ireland, replacing the use of internment with imprisonment after trial for specific crimes. Also, responsibility for policing was increasingly shifted from British soldiers back to the RUC, aided by the locally recruited UDR. These policies brought new problems. Despite Britain's best efforts, the RUC and the UDR were overwhelmingly Protestant forces. The UDR in particular failed to win the confidence of Catholics, who correctly claimed that some UDR soldiers had connections with Loyalist paramilitaries. Off-duty UDR men were a favourite target for IRA assassination.

Alien oppression

While on hunger strike, IRA prisoner Bobby Sands issued a statement:

'I am a political prisoner because I am a casualty of a perennial war that is being fought between the oppressed Irish people and an alien, oppressive, unwarranted regime that refuses to withdraw from our land.'

He stood by 'the God-given right of the Irish nation to sovereign independence and the right of any Irishman or woman to assert this right in armed revolution.'

Hunger strikes

But it was the policy of 'criminalization' – treating the IRA and Protestant terrorists as straightforward criminals being punished under the law – that led to the next major crisis in Northern Ireland. After the introduction of internment, the British government had granted IRA and other paramilitary prisoners 'special category status', in effect recognizing them as political prisoners. This had allowed them many privileges commonly allowed to prisoners of war, but not found in ordinary jails. From 1976, this special status was progressively withdrawn.

From 1978, Republican prisoners held in the 'H-blocks' of the Maze prison staged protests against being treated as common criminals. In 1981, some of them went on hunger strike. The British government refused to make any concessions, and the first hunger striker, Bobby Sands, died on 5 May after refusing food for 66 days. Nine other prisoners died before the hunger strikes were called off in August.

Flanked by masked IRA men, the coffin of hunger striker Bobby Sands is carried in procession from his home to a nearby church, May 1981.

The deaths of the hunger strikers, especially of Bobby Sands, had a massive emotional impact on Irish Catholics. It was in

Moment of awakening

Gemma McHenry, a teenager in the Andersonstown district of Belfast when hunger striker Bobby Sands died, wrote later:

'I made the decision to attend the funeral of Bobby Sands. I would usually have stayed away from anything political, but I went as a sign of respect for a young man who had given his life for what he believed in. I did it as a sign of disgust at a government who had let it happen and didn't care about any of us ... This was an awakening for me. My usual life of school, boys and fashion faded away and for once in my life I knew how I felt ... I was an Irish Catholic Nationalist and it was important to me.'
(Quoted in Holliday, *Children of "the Troubles"*)

vain that opponents of the IRA pointed out the deaths caused by the organization to which Sands belonged – for example, there were 30 members of the security forces killed in IRA shootings and bombings during the period of the hunger strikes. Most Catholics saw only the courageous sacrifice of the prisoners and the apparent heartlessness of the British government. There was a flood of fresh support for the Republican cause. During the hunger strike, Sands was elected to the Westminster parliament, defeating a prominent Unionist in a by-election in Fermanagh-South Tyrone. Two hunger strikers were also elected to the Irish parliament.

A Republican mural attempts to draw a parallel between the IRA's fight against British rule in Northern Ireland and the struggle against apartheid in South Africa led by Nelson Mandela and the ANC.

These and other election successes for Republicans were an unexpected, but in the long term very important, result of the hunger strikes. Sinn Fein, the political wing of the IRA, had played only a minor role in the Troubles. All the IRA's efforts had been focused on the armed struggle. But as Sinn Fein candidates began to score successes, the IRA adopted a new strategy combining a search for votes with military action. One leading Republican asked an IRA conference in 1981: 'Will anyone here object if, with a ballot paper in one hand and the Armalite [rifle] in the other, we take power in Ireland?'

Over the following decade, led by Gerry Adams, Sinn Fein stopped being simply a mouthpiece for the IRA. Dedicated to winning Catholic votes, it developed an interest in distancing itself from bombings and shootings, which could lose it the support of thousands of voters. Unionists insisted that Sinn Fein had always been, and essentially continued to be, the political wing of the IRA. But it was also true that Sinn Fein's participation in democratic politics offered a glimmer of hope for peace.

THE SEARCH FOR PEACE

In the 1980s and early 1990s, there was no sign of any possible peaceful resolution of the Northern Ireland conflict. IRA operations in mainland Britain continued. The most spectacular of many attacks was the bombing of a hotel in Brighton during the Conservative Party conference of 1983, which narrowly failed to kill Prime Minister Margaret Thatcher. In Northern Ireland, the worst atrocity of this period was when an IRA bomb planted at the Enniskillen war memorial killed 11 local people on Remembrance Sunday 1987.

Living with fear

In April 1994, a man was shot outside the house where 11-year-old Catholic Bridie Murphy lived in West Belfast. The following day she wrote in her diary:

'I am frightened living on this street across from the Protestants. I am frightened they will come and kill us because this is the eleventh time they have shot people in our street. I don't know why they want to kill us.'
(Quoted in Holliday, *Children of "the Troubles"*)

The centre of Enniskillen was bombed minutes before a Remembrance ceremony was to take place, for soldiers killed in the two world wars.

OUR GLORIOUS DEAD
1914-1918
1939-1945

Turning away from the IRA

A middle-aged Belfast Catholic, who was impressed by the IRA when he was a young man, told an interviewer in the 1990s that they had become an embarrassment:

'I have no time for the IRA, they make nothing but trouble for Catholics now. I worked for a while in Stewartstown, with Protestants all around me. When an IRA thing happened, you hated to hear it, because of all the comments you'd get, and what could you say?'
(Quoted in O'Connor, *In Search of a State*)

But the most graphic display of the apparently endless cycle of violence came in March 1988. First, three IRA members preparing a car-bomb attack were shot dead by British special forces in Gibraltar. Then the funeral for the IRA bombers was attacked by a Loyalist gunman, killing three mourners. And during the funeral for those three victims, two British soldiers were dragged out of a car and murdered by a Republican crowd. No wonder many people were inclined to despair.

Changing times

Yet significant changes were under way. Firstly, Britain's relationship with the Irish Republic was improving, partly because, since 1973, both countries had been part of the European Community (now the European Union). In 1985 the British and Irish governments signed an Anglo-Irish Agreement, which basically recognized that the Republic had a right to be consulted about what happened in Northern Ireland. In return, the Republic agreed to improve cooperation in security operations against the IRA. Unionists were predictably outraged, but their protests were firmly contained by the RUC.

Irish president Mary Robinson addresses the European Parliament, May 1995.

Changing attitudes and rising living standards in the Republic were beginning to lessen differences with Northern Ireland. Since the 1960s, the southern Irish had become far more prosperous. In the 1990s, under the presidency of Mary Robinson, conservative Catholic attitudes in the Republic came under attack. Robinson also encouraged a new sympathetic attitude to Ulster Protestants, going so far as to condemn the Anglo-Irish Agreement for infringing Protestant rights.

In the early 1990s there was an outbreak of talks. The Catholic SDLP talked to the Protestant Unionist parties; SDLP leader John Hume held talks with Sinn Fein's Gerry Adams; and the British government (while publicly claiming not to negotiate with terrorists) held secret talks with the IRA. The upshot was a major peace initiative in 1993. Reaching out to the Catholic nationalists, the British government issued the 'Downing Street declaration'. This stated that Britain had 'no selfish strategic or economic interest in Northern Ireland' – in other words, all Britain wanted was an agreement that would satisfy all sides, and if that meant Northern Ireland ceased to be part of the United Kingdom, so be it.

At the same time, an effort was made to allay Protestant fears. The Irish government publicly stated that it would be wrong to impose a united Ireland against the will of the Protestant majority in the North. Also, the SDLP and Sinn Fein agreed that it was necessary, or at least desirable, to persuade Protestants to consent to a united Ireland, rather than imposing it on them. This was an important step forward, reflecting a genuine effort by many Catholic nationalists to understand the Protestant point of view. With the Unionists ready to consider concessions in return for an end to the IRA campaign, peace talks now seemed possible.

SDLP leader John Hume (left) and Gerry Adams, head of Sinn Fein, at a press conference in New York, February 1994.

15 December 1993: British prime minister John Major (left) and Irish prime minister Albert Reynolds present the 'Downing Street Declaration'.

Ending the nightmare

Protestant mother Joyce Cathcart wrote during the IRA ceasefire of 1994-96:

'Each day without a life being taken is a bonus. I now have a two-and-a-half-year-old daughter and another baby on the way. For their sake I want peace. No principle is worth spilling another drop of Ulster blood for. Life is precious; the nightmare has gone on long enough.'
(Quoted in Holliday, *Children of "the Troubles"*)

Fragile peace

In August 1994, the IRA announced that they were ending their military campaign. This was widely hailed as an historic end to violence. When Gerry Adams visited the USA, he was greeted as a peacemaker and was invited to the White House by President Bill Clinton. But Unionists remained sceptical, pointing out that the IRA still had their weapons. Of course, Loyalist paramilitaries, who had been killing about 40 people a year in the early 1990s, also remained fully armed. The British government supported the Unionists' view that Sinn Fein could not take part in peace talks until the IRA had disarmed, 'decommissioning' their weapons.

President Bill Clinton was the first serving US president to visit Northern Ireland.

At Christmas 1995 President Clinton visited both Catholic and Protestant areas of Northern Ireland in a gesture of American support for the peace process. But by then storm clouds were already gathering once more. In February 1996, impatient at

the lack of progress towards including Sinn Fein in peace talks, the IRA ended the truce in spectacular fashion, exploding a huge bomb at Canary Wharf, in London's Docklands area. Other bombings followed, including one that destroyed the centre of Manchester. In July, Northern Ireland was torn apart by renewed sectarian violence, after Protestant Orangemen were banned from marching to Drumcree through a Catholic area of Portadown. Across the province Protestant mobs fought with police and attacked Catholic homes. When the police backed down and allowed the Drumcree march to proceed, Catholics rioted. Peace was in tatters.

11 July 1996: a Catholic woman argues with Protestant Orangemen on their controversial annual Drumcree march through the Garvaghy Road in Portadown.

12 July 1996: a Catholic area of Belfast after the riots that followed the Drumcree march.

Yet, surprisingly, the peace process continued through the mayhem. In May 1996 the people of Northern Ireland elected an all-party forum, or assembly, where peace talks were to take place. An American senator, George Mitchell, was appointed to chair the talks. Voters elected 17 Sinn Fein representatives to the forum, but they were not allowed to take their seats because of the continuing IRA violence. Without Sinn Fein, little progress could be made.

US Senator George Mitchell chaired the 21-month-long talks that resulted in a peace agreement.

May 1998: Mo Mowlam, secretary of state for Northern Ireland (left) talks to people in Belfast as she campaigns for a 'yes' vote in the referendum on the Good Friday Agreement.

In May 1997, a general election in Britain brought the New Labour government led by Tony Blair to office. He appointed the unconventional Mo Mowlam as Secretary for Northern Ireland. Mowlam's directness and evident goodwill brought a new momentum to the peace process. In July the IRA once more declared a ceasefire and Sinn Fein were allowed to join the peace talks – the issue of decommissioning was postponed. The new British government believed that peace was only possible if all parties, including paramilitaries, were included in any deal. Sinn Fein leaders Gerry Adams and Martin McGuinness were invited to meet the prime minister in Downing Street, and Mowlam went for talks with Loyalist paramilitary prisoners inside the Maze prison. When the IRA broke the ceasefire with a murder in February 1998, Sinn Fein were only banned from the talks for a fortnight.

Good Friday agreement

Under intense pressure from Tony Blair, his Irish opposite number Bertie Ahern, and President Clinton, the Northern Ireland parties reached an agreement on Good Friday, 10 April 1998. There was to be a Northern Ireland parliament elected by proportional representation and a power-sharing executive committee – a government chosen from all parties in the parliament, including Sinn Fein. The Irish Republic was to be involved in the North through various bodies, but it would change its constitution to end its claim to rule the province. The RUC was to be reformed to become a truly non-sectarian police force. Controversially, all prisoners convicted of terrorist offences were to be released within two years. Arrangements were to be made for the paramilitaries to give up their weapons.

10 April 1998: British prime minister Tony Blair (seated left) and Irish prime minister Bertie Ahern sign the peace agreement.

The British and Irish governments hastily held referendums to confirm popular support for the peace accord. In the Irish Republic, an overwhelming 94 per cent of votes cast were in favour of the agreement. In Northern Ireland it won the support of a substantial majority – 71 per cent voted 'yes', more than two out of three. But the agreement was far more popular with Catholics

23 May 1998: a 'yes' campaigner shows off the results of the referendum.

From war to politics

At the time of the referendum on the Good Friday peace agreement, journalist Mary Holland, who had covered the Ulster conflict for 30 years, wrote:

'Now is the time when the people of Northern Ireland can sense the possibility of a new beginning, a new politics which could allow both communities to live at ease with each other. The Yes vote may make it possible to move from the most intractable of conflicts to politics – the conduct of war by other means.'
(*The Irish Times*, 11 April 1998)

than Protestants, who were split almost evenly for and against. Unionists opposed to the agreement, including the Orange Order, denounced it as a surrender to the IRA.

In June 1998 elections were held and the following month pro-agreement Unionist leader David Trimble became Northern Ireland's first minister. However, anti-agreement Unionists won as many seats as Trimble's supporters. In the first two weeks of July Loyalists opposed to the agreement orchestrated a campaign of violence centred around the annual Drumcree march. While members of the Orange Order

Joining hands across the divide: after his election as first minister, Unionist David Trimble (right) poses for the press with his deputy, Seamus Mallon of the SDLP.

confronted the security forces across barricades at Portadown, Loyalists set up roadblocks and carried out attacks on Catholic homes across the province. On 12 July, a house in Ballymoney, County Antrim, was petrol-bombed by Loyalist paramilitaries during the night. Three young children were burned to death in the blaze.

There was also opposition to the agreement among Republicans. The IRA flatly refused to contemplate decommissioning weapons. Some IRA members went further. Feeling that the Republican cause had been betrayed, a splinter group calling itself the Real IRA began carrying out car-bombings in an attempt to disrupt the peace process. On 15 August they hit Omagh.

In the wake of the Omagh massacre, Gerry Adams made a strong statement declaring that violence in Northern Ireland must be 'a thing of the past, over, done with, and gone'. Some Unionist leaders had made similar statements after the killing of the three children in County Antrim. But in the aftermath of these shocking events, it remained unclear whether peace was really on the horizon, or whether a new phase in the conflict was about to begin.

PROBLEMS AND PROSPECTS

The 1998 Nobel Peace Prize was awarded jointly to John Hume of the SDLP and David Trimble of the Ulster Unionists. But it remained desperately difficult to implement the Good Friday agreement. For the agreement to work, the Unionists had to sit with Sinn Fein members in a Northern Ireland executive. Pro-agreement Unionists accepted to do this, but on condition that the IRA disarmed. The IRA, however, refused to give up their weapons, although they eventually agreed to allow weapons dumps to be inspected.

2 February 2000: graffiti in a village in South Armagh seems an expression of the IRA's refusal to disarm.

After further lengthy negotiations, a power-sharing executive at last began a precarious on-off existence in December 1999, but the Unionists were reluctant participants.

Weapons inspections were a short term solution and the Provisional IRA failed to decommission. This led to David Trimble resigning on 1 July 2001 in protest. However, after the terrorist attack on the World Trade Centre in New York on September 11 2001, international pressure increased on the Provisional IRA and they began the process of putting arms beyond use. This was verified by The Independent International Commission on Decommissioning and David Trimble was satisfied and reelected as First Minister on 6 November 2001. However, some unionists weren't satisfied and decommissioning remains an obstacle to the peace process.

Continuing violence

Meanwhile the release of convicted terrorists went ahead. The spectacle of murderers going free after serving only part – and in some cases a small part – of

Punishment beating

In the 1990s, a young Catholic living in Derry was repeatedly subjected
to IRA 'punishment beatings' because of his involvement in petty crime.
He told an interviewer:

'First time they wanted me to leave the country, I was only 13. They
took me away for six hours and burnt me with fags. They struck me
with a soldering iron bar and made me kneel down for six hours and
battered the back of me with a bat, while I had a hood over my head.
They were threatening to take me and shoot me dead, and bury me ...
The people that done this to me are definitely scumbags.'
(Quoted in Smythe and Faye ed., *Personal Accounts from Northern
Ireland's Troubles*)

their sentence filled many people with disquiet. In some areas
of Northern Ireland paramilitary violence remained a feature of
everyday life. In some Catholic districts, IRA vigilantes still
enforced their idea of justice, inflicting 'punishment beatings'
on petty criminals and ordering disruptive youths to leave the
country. In Protestant areas of Belfast, the release of Loyalist
prisoners in the summer of 2000 sparked a murderous feud

July 2000: convicted IRA
terrorists are released from
the Maze Prison, Belfast,
under the terms of the
Good Friday agreement.

No apologies

Michael Stone, a Loyalist paramilitary jailed for killing six people, gave a televised interview when he was released on 24 July 2000. He said his war was over, but:

'They were military operations ... Many of them were successful from a Loyalist paramilitary viewpoint ... I would be a hypocrite to say sorry.'
(Quoted in *The Times*, 25 July 2000)

between rival Loyalist paramilitary organizations which brought British soldiers back on to the streets. The paramilitary violence was often more to do with ordinary crime – protection rackets and drug-dealing – than with politics of any kind.

What was it for?

Jim McAllister, a Republican from South Armagh, expressed the mixed feelings that many activists have about a peace settlement:

'If it's over I suppose there could be a sense of relief in some way, but there must be an awful sadness too, because if it's over, what was it for?'
(Quoted in Harnden, *'Bandit Country'*)

Still, there was a large measure of peace, and life in most of Northern Ireland took on a more normal aspect with the dismantling of security. The new generation growing up in the province had, however, inevitably been marked by the experience of the conflict. In 2000, one in three teenagers said they had seen a person killed or seriously injured at some time in their lives. Catholic and Protestant children almost all still went to separate schools. Many groups worked patiently to break down barriers, for example organizing holiday activities for mixed groups of young Protestants and Catholics. But it was slow work.

Facing the future

The potential for a renewal of wholesale armed conflict in Northern Ireland remained real. Sinn Fein and the IRA had accepted the peace agreement as a stepping stone to the eventual unification of Ireland. If this seemed unlikely to be achieved, the IRA might resume their campaign. On the other hand, Unionists totally rejected a future in which they would become a minority in a unified Ireland. Protestants turned increasingly against the agreement as they were forced, as they saw it, to make so many concessions to Catholics without the IRA giving an inch.

Some striking attempts were made to settle past issues. An inquiry was set up to try to find out the truth about the 1972 Bloody Sunday deaths. And the IRA tried to return the bodies of victims they had abducted and killed – the 'disappeared'. But these efforts seemed only to stir up past memories rather than resolve them. Perhaps what the people of Northern Ireland really needed was to forget the past. Irish novelist James Joyce had one of his characters say: 'History is a nightmare from which I am trying to escape.' This could be applied to Northern Ireland.

Friends at the funeral of James Barker, Sean McCloughlin and Oran Doherty, who were killed in the Omagh bombing, 1998.

Poem for peace

Among those who died in the Omagh bombing in August 1998 was 12-year-old Sean McLaughlin. Ironically, along with a group of schoolfriends, Sean had won a poetry competition with a poem calling for peace between the 'orange' Protestants and the 'green' Catholics in Northern Ireland.

The poem read:
'Orange and green, it doesn't matter
United now, don't shatter our dream.
Scatter the seeds of peace
Over our land,
So we can travel hand in hand
Across the bridge of hope.'

DATE LIST

1603	The defeat of an Irish revolt opens the way for Protestant settlement in Ulster.
1 July 1691	Protestant William III defeats Catholic James II at the Battle of the Boyne.
1801	The Act of Union creates the United Kingdom of Great Britain and Ireland.
1845-50	Over a million Irish people die in the Great Famine.
24-29 April 1916	British army crushes Easter Uprising in Dublin, intended to create an Irish republic.
1919	Sinn Fein MPs form an Irish parliament, the Dail Eireann; the IRA begins a military campaign to end British rule.
December 1920	Britain passes Government of Ireland Act to set up a parliament in Belfast to run the six counties.
December 1921	The Anglo-Irish Treaty creates an Irish Free State controlling all of Ireland except the six counties.
1949	Ireland is declared a Republic and leaves the British Commonwealth.
1956	The IRA launches a 'border campaign' against British and Protestant rule in Northern Ireland; it ends in failure in 1962.
5 October 1968	Police clash with civil rights marchers in Londonderry.
4 January 1969	A People's Democracy march is attacked by Protestants at Burntollet Bridge, outside Derry.
12-15 August 1969	After violent clashes spread from Derry to Belfast, the British army is sent in to restore order.
6 February 1971	For the first time a British soldier is killed by the Provisional IRA.
9 August 1971	Internment is introduced in Northern Ireland.
30 January 1972	'Bloody Sunday': 14 people killed as British soldiers open fire after a demonstration in Londonderry.
24 March 1972	Britain imposes 'direct rule' on Northern Ireland, suspending the parliament at Stormont.
21 July 1972	On 'Bloody Friday' in Belfast, 9 people are killed and 130 injured by Provisional IRA bombs.
May 1974	A strike by Protestant workers forces the British government to abandon plans for a power-sharing executive in Northern Ireland; Protestant bombings kill 33 people in southern Ireland.
24 Nov. 1974	IRA bombings of two pubs in Birmingham kill 19 people.
Feb.-Nov. 1975	The IRA maintains a ceasefire; internment ends.
1976	Peace campaigners Mairead Corrigan and Betty Williams are awarded the Nobel Peace Prize.
27 August 1979	In two separate attacks, the IRA murder Earl Mountbatten and 3 other people in Sligo, and kill 19 British soldiers at Warrenpoint.
5 May 1981	IRA hunger striker Bobby Sands dies in the Maze prison.

1983	Sinn Fein leader Gerry Adams is elected MP for West Belfast.	**July 1997**	The IRA announces new ceasefire.
12 October 1984	The IRA bombs the Grand Hotel, Brighton, during the Conservative Party conference, narrowly failing to kill Prime Minister Thatcher.	**10 April 1998**	A peace agreement provides for a power-sharing executive in Northern Ireland which will include Sinn Fein.
November 1985	In the Anglo-Irish agreement, Britain recognizes that Dublin government has legitimate interest in the affairs of Northern Ireland.	**15 August 1998**	A 'Real IRA' car bomb kills 29 people in Omagh.
		December 1998	SDLP leader John Hume and Ulster Unionist leader David Trimble are jointly awarded the Nobel Peace Prize.
31 August 1994	IRA declares a ceasefire. It ends with bombing of Canary Wharf, London, on 9 February 1996.		
May 1996	An all-party forum is elected to negotiate a Northern Ireland settlement.	**2 December 1999**	A power-sharing executive is finally set up in Northern Ireland.

RESOURCES

FURTHER INFORMATION

Toby Harnden's book 'Bandit Country' is a readable inside story about the IRA's most intractable members in South Armagh – although be warned that it contains very gory details of atrocities. If you can find it, Laurel Holliday's Children of the Troubles gives an excellent insight into the feelings and experiences of people on all sides of the Northern Ireland conflict.

The Internet is an especially rich source of material on the conflict in Northern Ireland. Outstanding is the CAIN (Conflict Archive on the Internet) site on Northern Ireland at cain.ulst.ac.uk. It has extensive background information, as well as detailed coverage of major events and issues. Also recommended is the Irish Times site, www.ireland.com, which has a valuable feature section called 'Path to Peace'. The American broadcasting network PBS has graphic coverage of the history of the IRA and Sinn Fein at www.pbs.org/wgbh/pages/frontline/shows/ira.

To find outspoken statements of varying views of the Northern Ireland conflict, try the websites of the major political parties: the Ulster Unionists at www.uup.org; the Democratic Unionists at www.dup.org.uk; Sinn Fein at www.sinnfein.ie; and the SDLP at www.sdlp.ie.

SOURCES

Sources of information for this book were:
Tim Pat Coogan, The IRA, Fontana, London, 1980
R. F. Foster, Modern Ireland 1600-1972, Penguin, 1988
Toby Harnden, 'Bandit Country': The IRA and South Armagh, Hodder & Stoughton, 1999
Thomas Hennessey, A History of Northern Ireland 1920-1996, Gill & Macmillan, 1997
Laurel Holliday, Children of "The Troubles": Our Lives in the Crossfire of Northern Ireland, Washington Square Press, 1997
Keith Jeffery ed., The Divided Province: The Troubles in Northern Ireland 1969-85, Orbis Publishing, 1985
Robert Kee, The World We Left behind: A Chronicle of the Year 1939, Weidenfeld and Nicholson, 1984
Nell McCafferty, Peggy Deery: A Derry Family at War, Attic Press, 1988
Fionnuala O'Connor, In Search of a State: Catholics in Northern Ireland, The Blackstaff Press, 1993
Ulick O'Connor, The Troubles, Arrow Books, 1997
Cormac Ó Grada, The Great Irish Famine, Cambridge University Press, 1989
Marie Smythe and Marie-Therese Fay ed., Personal Accounts from Northern Ireland's Troubles, Pluto Press, 2000
Peter Somerville-Large, Irish Voices: An Informal History 1916-66, Pimlico, 2000

GLOSSARY

B-Specials — a force of armed part-time Protestant policemen in Northern Ireland, disbanded in 1970; it was hated by Catholics for its alleged brutality.

Dail Eireann — the Irish parliament.

decommiss-ioning — handing over stocks of weapons and ammunition or putting them out of use.

Dissenter — a member of one of the Protestant groups that reject the authority of the Church of England (also known as Non-Conformists).

dominion — a state forming part of the British Empire but having its own independent government.

Fenian — The Fenians were a secret organization set up in the 1850s to fight for Irish independence; the word is often used by Northern Ireland Protestants for any Catholic nationalist.

Gaelic — the language of the Celtic people of Ireland and Scotland.

Good Friday agreement — agreement reached on 10 April 1998 between the Northern Ireland political parties, intended to end the Northern Ireland conflict.

Home Rule — proposal under which Ireland would have had its own government, but would have remained a part of the United Kingdom.

internment — detention without charge or trial, usually in a camp rather than a prison.

loyalist — essentially the same as a 'Unionist', but usually employed for members or supporters of the more extreme Protestant organizations.

nationalist — in Northern Ireland, someone who believes that all of Ireland should be united under the Dublin government; often used simply to mean 'Catholic'.

Orange Order — Protestant organization in Northern Ireland dedicated to resisting Catholicism and upholding Ulster Protestant traditions.

paramilitary — belonging to an armed organization that is not part of a regular army or police force.

power-sharing executive — governing body for Northern Ireland in which opposing political parties take part.

province — 'The province' is a term often used to refer to Northern Ireland.

Republican — In Northern Ireland, a member or supporter of Sinn Fein, the IRA, or other similar organizations; confusingly, Republicans are generally hostile to the government of the Irish Republic.

sectarian — motivated by hostility towards a group of people holding different religious beliefs.

the 'Troubles' — a term once used for the fighting in Ireland from 1919 to 1923, but now used to refer to the events in Northern Ireland since 1969.

Ulster — one of the four provinces of Ireland; six of the nine counties of Ulster became Northern Ireland.

Unionist — a person or political group that believes in keeping Northern Ireland as part of the UK.

vigilantes — people who take it upon themselves to suppress criminal activity of which they disapprove.

INDEX

ABBREVIATIONS

IRA	Irish Republican Army
IRB	Irish Republican Brotherhood
NICRA	Northern Ireland Civil Rights Association
PD	People's Democracy
RUC	Royal Ulster Constabulary
SDLP	Social Democratic and Labour Party
UDA	Ulster Defence Association
UDR	Ulster Defence Regiment
UN	United Nations
UVF	Ulster Volunteer Force